570

✓

Puddle Jumper

Many thanks to Sarah, Barry, and Claire:
The Dirt Road people who shared their time,
thoughtfulness, and good will.

Text copyright © 1993 by Ann Morris
Photographs copyright © 1993 by Ken Heyman
All rights reserved. No part of this book may be reproduced or utilized in any form or by any means, electronic or mechanical, including photocopying and recording, or by any information storage and retrieval system, without permission in writing from the Publisher. Inquiries should be addressed to Lothrop, Lee & Shepard Books, a division of William Morrow & Company, Inc., 1350 Avenue of the Americas, New York, New York 10019. Printed in the United States of America.

First Edition   1   2   3   4   5   6   7   8   9   10

Library of Congress Cataloging in Publication
Morris, Ann, Puddle jumper / Ann Morris ; photographs by Ken Heyman.
    p.   cm.   Summary: A young girl helps her father as he develops his idea for a new wooden toy and then builds it.
ISBN 0-688-10204-2. — ISBN 0-688-10205-0 (lib. bdg.)   1. Wooden toy making—Juvenile literature.   [1. Toy making.
2. Woodwork.]   I. Heyman, Ken, ill.   II. Title.   TT174.5.W6M67   1993   745.592—dc20   92-14763   CIP   AC

Puddle Jumper

◆ HOW A TOY IS MADE ◆

BY ANN MORRIS ◆ PHOTOGRAPHS BY KEN HEYMAN

LOTHROP, LEE & SHEPARD BOOKS
NEW YORK

Sarah's dad, Barry, is a toymaker. He makes wooden toys for children to ride on. Barry's workshop is near their home, and he likes Sarah to visit him while he works. She is a good helper.

Barry has an idea for a new toy he wants to build, a rocking airplane he calls the Puddle Jumper. First he draws his idea on paper. He figures out how big the toy will be and how it will fit together.

Then he makes a model to make sure the new toy will look and work as he imagined. It does! Now Barry is ready to build lots of Puddle Jumpers.

It takes plenty of wood to build rocking toys. Sarah goes with her dad to their lumber storage yard. They want to use only boards without knotholes, so they check each piece carefully.

Back in the workshop, Barry puts the long boards into
the planer to make them flat and even.

He decides to start with the wings. First he measures and draws a pattern on the wood, then he checks his measurements again to be sure they are correct.

Sarah checks her measurements twice before she starts to cut, too. She wants to be a good woodworker like her dad.

This router cuts through the top board, but not the bottom pattern board, so Barry can use his pattern again and again.

The wings' edges are jagged and full of splinters. Barry uses a shaper to round them off.

Then he sands the wood satin-smooth with a drum sander.

The finished wings are now ready to be decorated. Barry forces red paint through a silk screen to print designs on the wood. When all the wings are done, he will make the other parts of the plane, one by one.

At last, all the Puddle Jumper parts have been cut and painted and are ready to be put together.

The propeller goes on last.

Barry and Sarah pack up the airplanes. But before the new toys are sent to stores...

Sarah takes the Puddle Jumper for a test ride.